# Blessings for the Backpack of the Soul

Words of Inspiration for Pilgrims on the Way

## *Bendiciones para la mochila del alma*

*Palabras de inspiración para peregrinos en camino*

Edited by G. Christopher Clark

*Blessings for the Backpack of the Soul:*
*Words of Inspiration for Pilgrims on the Way*
Edited by G. Christopher Clark

Copyright © 2020 G. Christopher Clark
Published by G. Christopher Clark
ISBN: 978-1-71676-112-6

Cover art & page design by Chris Clark (www.gchrisclark.com)
Laid out in Adobe InDesign, using Open Sans & Adobe Caslon Pro

First edition

For Sister Macrina Wiederkehr

July 28, 1939 – April 24, 2020

"May you carry your joy and your grief
in the backpack of your soul."

*«Que lleves tu alegría y tu aflicción
en la mochila de tu alma».*

# Table of Contents

## Modern Prayers

## Song Lyrics

## Poetry

## Afterword

## Credits

## Additional Works

## Acknowledgments

Foreword

by Salvatore Sapienza

Throughout the centuries, mystics and saints — regardless of faith or wisdom tradition — have pointed towards "The Way."

In the 4th century BC, Lao Tzu wrote the Tao te Ching, which means "Book of the Way." Two thousand years ago, Jesus of Nazareth instructed his disciples to follow "The Way." And, for centuries now, spiritual pilgrims from all across the globe have gone to Spain to journey along *El Camino de Santiago*, "The Way of St, James."

So, where exactly does "The Way" lead? Asia? The Holy Land? Santiago de Compostela?

What Lao Tzu, Jesus, and Camino pilgrims have all discovered is that "The Way" is not an outer journey, but an inner one. There are many different spiritual paths, yet they all lead to the same destination: discovery of the Divinity within.

Lao Tzu wrote, "At the center of your being lies the answer." Jesus said, "The Kingdom of Heaven is within you." And, pilgrims along the Camino soon discover that the yellow wayfinding arrows are actually guiding them within. The Camino is an interior journey — the journey of the heart, leading one deeper into the soul.

You may be reading this on a pilgrimage, in preparation, or just out of curiosity. Whatever your situation as you start reading, let us pray:

# Walking "The Way"

Spirit of Love,
lead us and guide our steps
as we continue our walk along
the spiritual path and the journey of life.

May we be ever mindful
that we do not walk alone,
for we are being Divinely guided along the way,
always and in all ways.

With each step,
lead us deeper into the depths of the Soul
and the discovery of the Light within.

Amen.

Salvatore Sapienza


# Recorriendo «el Camino»

Espíritu del Amor,
guíanos y guía nuestros pasos
mientras seguimos nuestro caminar por
el sendero espiritual y el viaje de la vida.

Seamos siempre conscientes
de que no caminamos solos,
porque somos guiados Divinamente por el camino,
siempre y en todos los sentidos.

Con cada paso,
guíanos más a fondo hacia las profundidades del Alma
y al descubrimiento de la Luz interior.

Amén.

Salvatore Sapienza

# Introduction

La ruta nos aportó otro paso natural.

(Spanish palindrome)

*The route provided us another natural path.*

## About the Camino

I hope this book will appeal to all kinds of pilgrims, but I expect many will acquire it because of an interest in The Way of St. James (*El Camino de Santiago*). The Camino is a network of routes that lead to Santiago de Compostela in Spain's autonomous community of Galicia. Tradition has it that the remains of the Christian apostle St. James are buried there.

Religious pilgrims have walked the Camino for more than a thousand years, butir has recently begun to appeal to a wider audience — nearly 350,000 = in 2019! The most popular route is the *Camino Francés* (map below), starting just inside the French border, covering 478 miles, and typically taking at least thirty days to complete on foot.

Medieval pilgrims collected a shell in Santiago to prove they had made the journey. Today a scallop shell is worn en route as a sort of identity badge; when bystanders see it they greet the wearer with "Buen Camino!" Besides the shell, two other symbols are closely tied to the Camino: the red cross of the Order of Santiago and bright yellow wayfinding arrows.

The traditional resting place each night is an albergue, a modest hostel where pilgrims donate a small fee in exchange for a place to sleep.

Modern pilgrims who obtain a *credencial* (Camino passport) and have it stamped along the way can receive a certificate when they arrive at the Cathedral in Santiago. One must walk at least 100 kilometers to earn this *Compostela*.

# About this book

This project grew out of a wish to have food for thought to sustain me during a month of walking the Camino. I noticed people sharing poems and prayers on Camino websites, so I collected them and then conducted an extended search for additional material. I assembled everything into a format that I could easily read on my phone and, when I stood back, it struck me that this was something I would want to share.

I decided on two pilgrim-friendly formats: a paperback to tuck into a backpack and an e-book to carry on a mobile device. To stay within copyright laws, I secured permission from authors. My plan all along was for the book to earn me nothing and cost only time, so the paper version sells at cost and downloads are free.

I have tried to make the book inclusive and have it appeal to a wide audience. There is material from from every continent and many religious traditions, representing diverse ways of knowing. The *Credits* section is more than a simple list of permissions; it provides a picture of diversity along with surprising details. I believe it's worth a read.

# About the translations

The book makes it easy for English-speaking pilgrims to share inspiration with the locals in a Spanish-speaking area. Most of the pieces are followed by translations, with the original (Spanish or English) always presented first.

The translations are literal; in the poems and songs I did not try to recreate rhyme or rhythm. In some cases, inclusive language and modernized wording have been substituted.

I wrote all of the translations that are not otherwise credited. I received a great deal of help (see *Acknowledgments*), but any remaining errors and awkwardness are mine.

# Ancient Words

Do justice, love mercy,
and walk humbly with your God.

(Micah 6:8)

*Haz justicia, ama la misericordia,
y camina humildemente con tu Dios.*

# Dum Pater Familias

Dum pater familias, Rex universorum,
Donaret provincias Ius apostolorum,
Jacobus Yspanias lux illustrat morum.

Primus ex apostolis, martir Jerosolimis,
Jacobus egregio sacer est martyrio.

Jacobi Gallecia opem rogat piam
Plebe cuius gloria dat insignem viam,
Ut precum frequentia cantet melodiam:

Herru Sanctiagu grot Sanctiagu,
E ultreya e suseya, Deus aia nos.

*Codex Calixtinus*

**Ultreya et suseya** *(roughly "onward and upward")* —
*various spellings of this phrase are seen along the Camino and
it is sometimes used responsively as a greeting among pilgrims.*

# When God the Father

When God the Father, King of the universe,
Was distributing territories among the apostles,
He assigned James to bring the light to Spain.

First among apostles, martyred in Jerusalem,
Peerless James was sanctified by his martyrdom.

The Galicia of James prays for pious tribute
From the people for whose glory it gives a famous path,
That in frequent prayer they might sing the melody:

"Lord Saint James, great Saint James,
Onward and upward, God speed our way!"

*Codex Calixtinus*


# Cuando Dios Padre

Cuando Dios Padre, Rey del universo,
Distribuía los territorios entre sus apóstoles,
Escogió a Santiago para ilustrar España.

Primero entre los apóstoles, martirizado en Jerusalén,
El insigne Santiago fue santificado en su martirio.

La Galicia de Santiago ruega piadoso tributo
Al pueblo para cuya gloria da insigne camino,
Que con abundancia de preces cante la melodía:

— ¡Oh señor Santiago, gran Santiago,
Adelante y arriba, que Dios nos proteja! —

*Codex Calixtinus*

# Tú eres el camino

Oh Dios, permite al espíritu elevarse hasta su augusta sede.
Concédele contemplar la fuente del bien.
Concédele, una vez hallada de nuevo la luz,
fijar en Ti la clara mirada del alma.

Disipa las nubes y el lastre de esta masa terrena
y brilla en tu esplendor;
pues Tú eres el cielo sereno,
Tú el reposo y la paz de los justos.

Contemplarte a ti es nuestro fin,
Tú eres a la vez principio, conductor y guía,
Tú el camino y el fin de nuestro viaje.

San Severino Boecio


# You are the Pathway

O God, let my spirit rise to its august seat.
May it contemplate the source of all goodness.
After the light is found once more,
May it fix on You the clear gaze of the soul.

Break through the mists and the weight of this Earth
and shine forth in Your splendor;
for You are calm weather,
You, the peaceful resting place of faithful souls.

To contemplate You is our goal,
You carry us and You go before,
You are the pathway and our journey's end.

St. Severinus Boëthius

# Nada te turbe

Nada te turbe,
Nada te espante,
Todo se pasa,
Dios no se muda.
La paciencia todo lo alcanza;
Quien a Dios tiene
Nada le falta:
Solo Dios basta.

Santa Teresa de Ávila

# Let Nothing Disturb You

Let nothing disturb you,
Let nothing frighten you,
All things pass:
God never changes.
Patience achieves everything.
Whoever has God
Lacks nothing:
God alone is enough.

St. Teresa of Avila

The remaining material in this chapter is presented in English first.
Several items do not include Spanish translations.

# Canticle of the Sun

Be praised, my Lord, through all Your creatures,
especially through Brother Sun,
through whom You bring the day and illuminate us.
He is beautiful and radiant in all his splendor!
Of You, Most High, he bears the likeness.

Praised be You, my Lord, through Sister Moon and the stars.
In heaven You formed them — clear and precious and beautiful.

Praised be You, my Lord, through Brother Wind,
and through the air, the cloud, and the calm sky,
and every kind of weather through which
You give sustenance to Your creatures.

Praised be You, my Lord, through Sister Water.
She is very humble, precious, and pure.

Praised be You, my Lord, through Brother Fire,
through whom You illuminate the night.
He is beautiful and bright and robust and strong.

Praised be You, my Lord, through our sister, Mother Earth,
who sustains us and governs us.
She produces diverse fruits, colorful flowers, and herbs.

Praised be You, my Lord,
through those who pardon for Your love's sake,
and suffer sickness and tribulation.
Blessed are they who suffer such things in peace
for by You, Most High, they will be crowned.

Praise and bless my Lord, and give thanks
and serve God with great humility.

St. Francis of Assisi

# Cántico de las criaturas

Alabado seas, mi Señor, en todas Tus criaturas,
especialmente en el hermano sol,
por quien nos das el día y nos iluminas.
¡Es bello y radiante con gran esplendor!
De Ti, Altísimo, lleva significación.

Alabado seas, mi Señor, en la hermana luna y las estrellas.
En el cielo las formaste claras y preciosas y bellas.

Alabado seas, mi Señor, en el hermano viento,
y en el aire y la nube y el cielo sereno,
y todo tipo de clima, por el cual
a Tus criaturas das sustento.

Alabado seas, mi Señor en la hermana agua.
Es muy humilde, preciosa y casta.

Alabado seas, mi Señor, en el hermano fuego,
por el cual iluminas la noche.
Es bello y alegre y vigoroso y fuerte.

Alabado seas, mi Señor, en la hermana nuestra madre Tierra,
que nos sostiene y gobierna.
Produce diversos frutos con coloridas flores y hierbas.

Alabado seas, mi Señor,
por aquellos que perdonan por Tu amor,
y sufren enfermedad y tribulación.
Bienaventurados los que las sufran en paz,
porque de Ti, Altísimo, coronados serán.

Alaben y bendigan a mi Señor y denle gracias
y sírvanle con gran humildad.

San Francisco de Asís

# The Deer's Cry

(St. Patrick's Breastplate)

I arise today
Through the strength of Heaven
Light of sun
Radiance of moon
Splendor of fire
Speed of lightning
Swiftness of wind
Depth of the sea
Stability of earth
Firmness of rock.

I arise today
Through God's strength to pilot me
God's eye to look before me
God's wisdom to guide me
God's way to lie before me
God's shield to protect me
From all who shall wish me ill
Afar and anear, alone and in a multitude
Against every cruel merciless power
That may oppose my body and soul.

Christ with me, Christ before me,
Christ behind me, Christ in me,
Christ beneath me, Christ above me,
Christ on my right, Christ on my left,
Christ when I lie down, Christ when I sit down,
Christ when I arise, Christ to shield me,
Christ in the heart of everyone who thinks of me,
Christ in the mouth of everyone who speaks of me.
I arise today.

St. Patrick

# Irish Blessing

May the road rise up to meet you.
May the wind be always at your back.
May the sun shine warm upon your face,
The rains fall soft upon your fields,
And until we meet again,
May God hold you in the palm of Their hand.

Traditional

# Bendición irlandesa

Que el camino se abra a tu encuentro.
Que el viento esté siempre a tu espalda.
Que el sol brille cálido sobre tu cara,
La lluvia caiga suave sobre tus campos,
Y hasta que volvamos a encontrarnos,
En la palma de su mano te sostenga Dios.

Tradicional

# The Song of Amergin

I am the wind on the sea;
I am the wave of the sea;
I am the bull of seven battles;
I am the eagle on the rock;
I am a flash from the sun;
I am the most beautiful of plants;
I am a strong wild boar;
I am a salmon in the water;
I am a lake in the plain;
I am the word of knowledge;
I am the head of the spear in battle;
I am the god that puts fire in the head;
Who spreads light in the gathering on the hills?
Who can tell the ages of the moon?
Who can tell the place where the sun rests?
Who, if not I?

Amergin Glúingel

# Today

I
Do not
Want to step so quickly
Over a beautiful line on God's palm
As I move through the earth's
Marketplace
Today.

I do not want to touch any object in this world
Without my eyes testifying to the truth
That everything is
My Beloved.

Something has happened
To my understanding of existence
That now makes my heart always full of wonder
And kindness.

I do not
Want to step so quickly
Over this sacred place on God's body
That is right beneath your
Own foot

As I
Dance with
Precious life
Today.

Hafiz

Translated by Daniel Ladinsky

# Lord, Be a Bright Flame

Lord, be a bright flame before me,
a guiding star above me,
a smooth path below me,
and a kindly shepherd behind me —
today, tonight, and forever.

St. Columba


# Señor, sé una llama luminosa

Señor, sé una llama luminosa ante mí,
sobre mí lucero que me guíe,
bajo mis pies senda suave,
tras de mí pastor bondadoso —
hoy, esta noche y siempre.

San Columba

# With Every Breath

With every breath I take today
I vow to be awake,
And every step I take
I vow to take with a grateful heart,
So I may see with the eyes of love
Into the hearts of all I meet,
To ease their burden when I can
And touch them with a smile of peace.

Buddhist prayer


# Con cada inhalación

Con cada inhalación que tomo hoy
Prometo estar despierto,
Y cada paso que doy
Prometo darlo con el corazón agradecido,
Para poder mirar con los ojos del amor
En los corazones de todos los que encuentro,
Para aliviar su carga cuando pueda
Y tocarlos con una sonrisa de paz.

Oración budista

# Traveler's Prayer

May it be Your will, Lord my God, to lead me to peace,
direct my steps to peace, and guide me to peace.

Rescue me from the hands of any enemy
or ambush along the way.

Send blessing to the work of my hands,
and let me find grace, kindness, and compassion
in Your eyes and in the eyes of all who see me.

Blessed are You, Lord, Who hears prayer.

*The Talmud*


# Plegaria del viajero

Sea Tu voluntad, Señor mi Dios, conducirme en paz,
dirigir mis pasos en paz, y guiarme en paz,

Sálvame de las manos de todo adversario
o emboscada por el camino.

Envía tu bendición a la obra de mis manos,
y concédeme gracia, bondad y compasión
en Tus ojos y en los ojos de todos quienes me vean.

Bendito eres Tú, Señor, que escuchas la plegaria.

*El Talmud*

# Prayer for Nature

Master of the Universe,
grant me the ability to be alone;
may it be my custom to go outdoors each day
among the trees and grass —
among all growing things
and there may I be alone,
and enter into prayer,
to talk with the One to whom I belong.

May I express there everything in my heart,
and may all the foliage of the field —
all grasses, trees, and plants —
awake at my coming,
to send the powers of their life
into the words of my prayer
so that my prayer and speech are made whole
through the life and spirit of all growing things,
which are made as one
by their transcendent Source.

May I then pour out the words of my heart
before your Presence like water, O Lord,
and lift up my hands to You in worship,
on my behalf, and that of my children!

Nachman of Breslov

# Morning and Evening Prayers

O God, You have let me pass the night in peace,
Let me pass the day in peace.

Wherever I may go upon my way,
Which You made peaceable for me,
O God, lead my steps.

When I am speaking, keep lies away from me.
When I am hungry, keep me from murmuring.
When I am satisfied, keep me from pride.

Calling upon You, I pass the day,
O lord who has no lord.

— — —

O God, You have let me pass the day in peace,
Let me pass the night in peace,
O lord who has no lord.

There is no strength but in You.
You alone have no obligation.

Under Your hand I pass the night.
You are my mother and my father.

The Boran People

## Oraciones de mañana y de noche

Oh Dios, me has dejado pasar la noche en paz
Permíteme pasar en paz el día.

Dondequiera que vaya en mi camino,
Que hiciste para mí pacífico,
Oh Dios, guía mis pasos.

Cuando esté hablando, apártame de las mentiras.
Cuando esté hambriento, no dejes que murmure.
Cuando esté satisfecho, aléjame del orgullo.

Invocándote paso el día,
Oh señor que no tiene señor.

— — —

Oh Dios, me has dejado pasar el día en paz
Permíteme pasar en paz la noche,
Oh señor que no tiene señor.

No hay fortaleza sino en Ti.
Solo Tú no tienes obligación alguna.

Bajo Tu mano paso la noche.
Eres mi madre y mi padre.

El pueblo Boran

# Song of the Sky Loom

Oh, our Mother the Earth,
Oh, our Father the Sky,
Your children are we, and with tired backs
We bring you the gifts that you love.

Then weave for us a garment of brightness.
May the warp be the bright light of morning;
May the fringes be the falling rain;
May the borders be the standing rainbow.

Thus weave for us a garment of brightness,
That we may walk fittingly where birds sing;
That we may walk fittingly where grass is green.
Oh, our Mother the Earth — oh, our Father the Sky.

*Tewa song*

# Canción del telar del cielo

Oh nuestra Madre la Tierra,
Oh nuestro Padre el Cielo.
Tus hijos somos y con las espaldas cansadas
Te traemos los regalos que amas.

Teje entonces para nosotros una prenda luminosa.
Que la urdimbre sea la luz brillante de la mañana;
Que los flecos sean la lluvia cayendo;
Que los bordes sean el arco iris luciente.

Teje así para nosotros una prenda luminosa,
Que caminemos apropiadamente donde cantan los pájaros;
Que caminemos apropiadamente donde la hierba es verde.
Oh nuestra Madre la Tierra, oh nuestro Padre el Cielo.

*Canción Tewa*

# Walking in Beauty

In beauty may I walk.
All day long may I walk.

Through the returning seasons may I walk.
On the trail marked with pollen may I walk.
With grasshoppers about my feet may I walk.
With dew about my feet may I walk.

With beauty may I walk.
With beauty before me may I walk.
With beauty behind me may I walk.
With beauty above me may I walk.
With beauty below me may I walk.
With beauty all around me may I walk.

In old age, wandering on a trail of beauty,
    lively, may I walk.
In old age, wandering on a trail of beauty,
    living again, may I walk.

It is finished in beauty.
It is finished in beauty.

Navajo prayer

*In this prayer and the following one, "to walk in beauty"
means to travel through life following the natural order, in
harmony with what surrounds you, recognizing its beauty and
connectedness. A Christian might call this a state of grace.*

# Great Spirit Prayer

Oh, Great Spirit,
whose voice I hear in the winds
and whose breath gives life to all the world,
Hear me!
I am small and weak.
I need your strength and wisdom.

Let me walk in beauty
and make my eyes ever behold
the red and purple sunset.
Make my hands respect the things you have made
and sharpen my ears to hear your voice.

Make me wise, so that I may understand
the things you have taught my people.
Let me learn the lessons you have hidden
in every leaf and rock.

Help me remain calm and strong
in the face of all that comes towards me.
Help me find compassion
without empathy overwhelming me.

I seek strength, not to be greater than my brother,
but to fight my greatest enemy: myself.
Make me always ready to come to you
with clean hands and straight eyes.

So, when life fades
as the fading sunset,
my spirit may come to you without shame.

Lakota prayer

# Oración al gran espíritu

Oh, Gran Espíritu,
cuya voz escucho en los vientos
y cuya respiración da vida a todo el mundo,
¡Escúchame!
Soy pequeño y débil.
Necesito tu fortaleza y tu sabiduría.

Déjame caminar en la belleza
y haz que mis ojos siempre contemplen
el rojo y el púrpura de la puesta del sol.
Haz que mis manos respeten las cosas que has creado
y aguza mis oídos para escuchar tu voz.

Hazme sabio para comprender
las cosas que has enseñado a mi pueblo.
Permíteme aprender las lecciones que has escondido
en cada hoja y cada piedra.

Ayúdame a mantener la calma y la fortaleza
ante todo lo que se me presente.
Ayúdame a encontrar la compasión
sin que la empatía me abrume.

Busco fortaleza, no para ser más que mi hermano,
sino para luchar contra mi peor enemigo: yo mismo.
Hazme estar siempre preparado para presentarme a ti
con las manos limpias y la mirada recta.

Para que, cuando la vida se desvanezca
como el sol en el ocaso,
mi espíritu pueda presentarse a ti sin vergüenza alguna.

Oración lakota

# Modern Prayers

Every time you leave home,
Another road takes you into a world you were never in.

(John O'Donohue)


*Cada vez que sales de casa,*
*Otro camino te adentra en un mundo en el que nunca estuviste.*

# Pilgrim Blessing

May flowers spring up where your feet touch the earth.
May the feet that walked before you bless your every step.
May the weather that's important
    be the weather of your heart.

May all of your intentions find their way
    into the heart of the Divine.
May your prayers be like flowers
    strewn for other pilgrims.
May your heart find meaning in unexpected events.

May friends who are praying for you carry you along the way.
May friends who are praying for you be carried in your heart.
May the circle of life encircle you along the way.

May the broken world ride on your shoulders.
May you carry your joy and your grief
    in the backpack of your soul.
May you remember all the circles of prayer
    throughout the world.

Macrina Wiederkehr

# Bendición del peregrino

Que broten flores donde tus pies tocan la tierra.
Que bendigan cada paso tuyo los pies que caminaron antes.
Que el clima importante
    sea el clima de tu corazón.

Que todas tus intenciones encuentren su camino
    hasta el corazón del Divino.
Que tus oraciones sean como flores
    esparcidas para otros peregrinos.
Que tu corazón encuentre significado en eventos inesperados.

Que los amigos que rezan por ti te lleven por el camino.
Que los amigos que rezan por ti vayan en tu corazón.
Que el círculo de la vida te circunde a lo largo del camino.

Que el mundo fracturado vaya sobre tus hombros.
Que lleves tu alegría y tu aflicción
    en la mochila de tu alma.
Que recuerdes todos los círculos de oración
    en el mundo entero.

Macrina Wiederkehr

# The Backpack of my Soul

At dawn, I try to prepare a light backpack,
Removing the weight of anxiety and self-doubt.
I make sure to have fresh food for the journey;
May it nourish me to wisdom and friendship.

On meeting the dawn's chill outside, I take out
Warm clothing to drive away bitterness and arrogance.
There's a map to help me find the way and
A guidebook that alerts me to the beauty of the path.

The contents of my pack sometimes surprise me:
Gems I forgot were there, or missing necessities.
But at the end of the day, when darkness approaches,
I know I can reach into its stillness and feel divine light.

G. Christopher Clark

# La mochila de mi alma

Al amanecer, intento preparar una mochila ligera,
Eliminando el peso de la ansiedad y la duda de mí mismo.
Me aseguro de tener comida fresca para el viaje;
Que me fomente en mi la sabiduría y la amistad.

Al encontrar ahí fuera el frío del alba, saco
Ropa cálida para alejar la amargura y la arrogancia.
Hay un mapa para ayudarme a encontrar el camino y
Una guía que me hace saber de la belleza del sendero.

El contenido de la mochila a veces me sorprende:
Gemas que olvidé que estaban allí, o necesidades perdidas.
Pero al final del día, cuando se acerca la oscuridad,
Sé que puedo buscar en su quietud y sentir la luz divina.

G. Christopher Clark

## Challenge Lover's Prayer

And let there be rain,
though the path is easier
when dry, and let there be
a bend in the road.
Let us think we know
where we are going —
and let us be wrong.
There are wings in us
we've forgotten.
Let us walk until
we remember them.
And then, let us walk
for the joy of walking.
Because puddles.
Because the path.

Rosemerry Wahtola Trommer


## Oración de la apasionada de los retos

Y que haya lluvia,
aunque el camino es más fácil
cuando está seco, y que haya
una curva en la senda.
Déjanos pensar que sabemos
adonde vamos —
y deja que nos equivoquemos.
Hay alas dentro de nosotros
de las que nos hemos olvidado.
Andemos hasta que
las recordemos.
Y luego, andemos
por la alegría de caminar.
Porque los charcos.
Porque el camino.

Rosemerry Wahtola Trommer

# Prayer for the Time of Sunrise

Blessed are you, Lord God of all Creation!
For the waning night and the rest it has brought us . . .
For the last star
    still shining as a guide into the new day . . .
For the small white moon
    high above my right shoulder,
    quietly fathering me along my way.
Blessed are you, Lord God of all Creation!
For the rising sun which will soon warm us . . .
For the sunflowers which raise their heads
    to greet the Creator in praise and admiration . . .
For the light which makes clear the way ahead . . .
For the pink and blue of the new sky,
    decorating the dawn with a bounty of color.

Blessed are you, Lord God of all Creation!
For the earth beneath my feet,
    an earth you welcome me to tread upon . . .
For the road stretching out before me and behind me . . .
For the thistles and reeds and weeds on its shoulders
    that keep me from wandering off the right path.
Blessed are you, Lord God of all Creation!
For my feet and legs and lungs . . .
For my heart, my soul, my mind . . .
    my family, my friends,
    all pilgrims on this road . . .
You have made us all.

Blessed, blessed, blessed are you,
Lord God of all Creation!

Kevin A. Codd

# Oración a la hora del amanecer

¡Bendito seas, Señor Dios de toda la Creación!
Por la noche menguante y el descanso que nos ha traído . . .
Por la última estrella
    aún luciendo como guía hacia el nuevo día . . .
Por la pequeña luna blanca
    bien alta sobre mi hombro derecho,
    guiándome tranquila y paternal en mi camino.
¡Bendito seas, Señor Dios de toda la Creación!
Por el sol naciente que pronto nos calentará . . .
Por los girasoles que levantan la cabeza
    en saludo de alabanza y admiración al Creador . . .
Por la luz que aclara el camino por recorrer . . .
Por el rosa y el azul del nuevo cielo,
    decorando el amanecer con profusión de colores.

¡Bendito seas, Señor Dios de toda la Creación!
Por la tierra bajo mis pies,
    tierra sobre la que me invitas a dejar mi huella . . .
Por el camino que se extiende delante y detrás de mí . . .
Por los cardos y cañas y maleza sobre los arcenes
    que me impiden desviarme del camino correcto.
¡Bendito seas, Señor Dios de toda la Creación!
Por mis pies y piernas y pulmones . . .
Por mi corazón, mi alma, mi mente . . .
    mi familia, mis amigos,
    todos los peregrinos en este camino . . .
Tú nos has hecho a todos.

¡Bendito, bendito, bendito seas,
Señor Dios de toda la Creación!

Kevin A. Codd

# Camino Call

Set out!
You were born for the road.

Set out!
You have a meeting to keep.

Where? With whom? You'll see.

Set out!
Your steps will be your words,
The road your song,
The weariness your prayers,
And at the end silence will speak to you.

Set out!
Your head does not know
Where your feet are leading your heart,
But the Guide will be with you,
Walking before you.

Set out!
You were born for the road,
The Pilgrim's road.
Someone is coming to meet you,
Seeking you in the shrine at the road's end,
In the shrine in the depths of your heart.
God is your peace.
God is your joy.

Go!
God walks with you.

Rick Zweck

# Llamada del Camino

¡Ponte en marcha!
Naciste para el camino.

¡Ponte en marcha!
Tienes que acudir a una reunión.

¿Dónde? ¿Con quién? Verás.

¡Ponte en marcha!
Tus pasos serán tus palabras,
El camino tu canción,
El cansancio tus oraciones,
Y al final el silencio te hablará.

¡Ponte en marcha!
La cabeza no sabe
Adonde los pies llevan al corazón,
Pero el Guía estará contigo,
Caminando delante de ti.

¡Ponte en marcha!
Naciste para el camino,
El camino del peregrino.
Alguien viene a conocerte,
Buscándote en el santuario del final del camino,
En el santuario de las profundidades de tu corazón.
Dios es tu paz.
Dios es tu alegría.

¡Ve!
Dios camina contigo.

Rick Zweck

# The Grasp of Your Hand

Let me not pray to be sheltered from dangers
but to be fearless in facing them.

Let me not beg for the stilling of my pain
but for the heart to conquer it.

Let me not look for allies in life's battlefield
but to my own strength.

Let me not crave, in anxious fear, to be saved
but hope for the patience to win my freedom.

Grant that I may not be a coward,
    feeling Your mercy in my success alone,
but let me find the grasp of Your hand in my failure.

Rabindranath Tagore

# Tu mano apretada

No pida yo nunca estar libre de peligros,
sino denuedo para afrontarlos.

No quiera yo que se apaguen mis dolores,
sino que sepa dominarlos mi corazón.

No busque yo amigos por el campo de batalla de la vida
sino más fuerza en mí.

No anhele yo, con afán temeroso, ser salvado
sino esperanza de conquistar, paciente, mi libertad.

No sea yo tan cobarde, Señor,
    que solo quiera Tu misericordia en mi triunfo,
sino que encuentre Tu mano apretada en mi fracaso.

Rabindranath Tagore

## May I Walk

May I walk this day in the realm of grace,
walking with You:
my feet firmly on Your earth-path,
my heart loving all as kindred,
my words and deeds alive with justice.

May I walk as blessing,
meeting blessing at every turn:
in every challenge, blessing,
in all opposition, blessing,
in harm's way, blessing.

May I walk each step in this moment of grace,
alert to hear You and awake enough
to say a simple "Yes."

Robert C. Morris

## Camine yo

Camine yo este día en el reino de la gracia,
andando contigo:
los pies firmes en Tu sendero de tierra,
amando de corazón a todos como una familia,
mis palabras y obras vivas y rectas.

Camine como bendición,
encontrando bendición a cada paso:
en cada desafío, bendición,
en toda oposición, bendición,
en riesgo de daño, bendición.

Camine cada paso en este momento de gracia,
atento para escucharte y lo bastante despierto
para decir un simple — Sí.—

Robert C. Morris

# A Prayer among Friends

Among other wonders of our lives, we are alive
with one another, we walk here
in the light of this unlikely world
that isn't ours for long.
May we spend generously
the time we are given.
May we enact our responsibilities
as thoroughly as we enjoy
our pleasures. May we see with clarity,
may we seek a vision
that serves all beings, may we honor
the mystery surpassing our sight,
and may we hold in our hands
the gift of good work
and bear it forth whole, as we
were borne forth by a power we praise
to this one Earth, this homeland of all we love.

John Daniel

## Una oración entre amigos

Entre otras maravillas de nuestras vidas, estamos vivos
unos con otros, caminamos aquí
a la luz de este mundo improbable
que no es nuestro por mucho tiempo.
Empleemos generosamente
el tiempo que se nos da.
Que cumplamos con nuestras responsabilidades
tan rigurosamente como disfrutamos
nuestros placeres. Que veamos con claridad,
que busquemos una visión
que sirva a todos los seres, que honremos
el misterio que supera nuestra vista
y que sostengamos en las manos
el don del trabajo bien hecho
y que lo llevemos adelante, como fuimos
llevados a luz por un poder que alabamos
a esta Tierra, esta patria de todo lo que amamos.

John Daniel

# A Mountaineer's Prayer

Gird me with the strength of Your steadfast hills,
The speed of Your streams give, too!
In the spirit that calms, with the life that thrills,
I would stand or run for You.
Let me be Your voice, or Your silent power,
As the waterfall, or the peak —
An eternal thought, in my earthly hour,
Of the living God to speak!

Clothe me in the rose-tints of Your skies,
Upon morning summits laid!
Robe me in the purple and gold that flies
Through Your shuttles of light and shade!
Let me rise and rejoice in Your smile aright,
As mountains and forests do!
Let me welcome Your twilight and Your night,
And wait for Your dawn anew!

Give me the brook's faith, joyously sung
Under clank of its icy chain!
Give me of the patience that hides among
The hill-tops, in mist and rain!
Lift me up from the dirt, let me breathe Your breath,
Your beauty and strength give, too!
Let me lose both the name and the meaning of death,
In the life that I share with You!

Lucy Larcom

## Pilgrim's Credo

I am not in control.
I am not in a hurry.
I walk in faith and hope.
I greet everyone with peace.
I bring back only what God gives me.

Murray Bodo


## Credo del peregrino

No estoy al mando.
No tengo prisa.
Camino con fe y esperanza.
Saludo a todos con paz.
Solo me llevo lo que Dios me da.

Murray Bodo

# On the Path to a Holy Well

Bless this path before us, Lord.
We come as pilgrims to walk in Your ways.
Help us to see the world as You do.
Help us to be quiet, to become still.
Let the rhythm of our walking help us
to tune our hearts
to the deeper rhythm of Your love.

Help us walk gently on the earth,
to give thanks for land, for water,
for all the wonders of Your creation.
We carry little for this journey
but we carry many burdens in our lives.
Help us with these; lighten our load.

We are going to a holy place,
following the footsteps of holy men and women
who went before us.
Help us to learn from them
and to find in our holy places
a spring of life-giving water for our own lives,
a place to come ever closer to You,
a place to help us know
the true goal of all our journeys.

Author unknown

## Camino a un pozo sagrado

Bendice el camino que tenemos por delante, Señor.
Venimos como peregrinos para recorrer Tus caminos.
Ayúdanos a ver el mundo como Tú lo ves.
Ayúdanos a estar callados, a tranquilizarnos.
Que el ritmo de nuestro andar nos ayude
a sintonizar nuestros corazones
con el ritmo profundo de Tu amor.

Ayúdanos a caminar ligero por el mundo,
a dar gracias por la tierra, por el agua,
por todas las maravillas de Tu creación.
Llevamos poco para este viaje
pero llevamos muchas preocupaciones en nuestras vidas.
Ayúdanos; alivia nuestra carga.

Vamos a un lugar sagrado,
siguiendo los pasos de hombres y mujeres santos
que pasaron antes que nosotros.
Ayúdanos a aprender de ellos
y a hallar en nuestros lugares sagrados
un manantial vivificante para nuestras propias vidas,
un lugar para acercarnos cada vez más a Ti,
un lugar para ayudarnos a conocer
la verdadera meta de todo viaje.

Autor desconocido

# For Those Who Have Far to Travel

If you could see
the journey whole,
you might never
undertake it,
might never dare
the first step
that propels you
from the place
you have known
toward the place
you know not.

Call it
one of the mercies
of the road:
that we see it
only by stages
as it opens
before us,
as it comes into
our keeping,
step by
single step.

There is nothing
for it
but to go,
and by our going
take the vows
the pilgrim takes:

to be faithful to
the next step;
to rely on more
than the map;
to heed the signposts
of intuition and dream;
to follow the star
that only you
will recognize;

to keep an open eye
for the wonders
that attend the path;
to press on
beyond distractions,
beyond fatigue,
beyond what would
tempt you
from the way.

There are vows
that only you
will know:
the secret promises
for your particular path
and the new ones
you will need to make
when the road
is revealed
by turns
you could not
have foreseen.

Keep them, break them,
make them again;
each promise becomes
part of the path,
each choice creates
the road
that will take you
to the place
where at last
you will kneel

to offer the gift
most needed—
the gift that only you
can give—
before turning to go
home by
another way.

Jan Richardson

# Father Mychal's Prayer

Lord, take me where You want me to go,
let me meet who You want me to meet,
tell me what You want me to say,
and keep me out of Your way.

Mychal Judge

# Oración del Padre Mychal

Señor, llévame adonde quieres que vaya,
hazme conocer a quien quieres que conozca,
dime lo que quieres que diga,
y no me dejes entorpecer Tu camino.

Mychal Judge

# Prayer for Travelers

This is a prayer for all the travelers.
For the ones who start out in beauty,
who fall from grace,
who step gingerly,
looking for the way back,

and for those who are born into the margins,
who travel from one liminal space to another,
crossing boundaries in search of center.

This is a prayer for the ones whose births
are a passing from darkness to darkness,
who all their lives are drawn toward the light,
and keep moving,

and for those whose journeys are a winding road
that begins and ends in the same place,
though only when the journey is completed
do they finally know where they are.

For all the travelers, young and old,
aching and joyful,
weary and full of life;
the ones who are here, and the ones who are not here;
the ones who are like you (and they're all like you)
and the ones who are different
(for in some ways, we each travel alone).

This is a prayer for traveling mercies,
and surefootedness,
for clear vision,
for bread
for your body and spirit,
for water,
for your safe arrival
and for everyone you see along the way.

Angela Herrera

# Oración para los viajeros

Esta oración es para todos los viajeros.
Para los que comienzan en la belleza
y caen de la gracia,
quienes caminan tímidamente,
buscando la manera de volver,

y para los que nacen en los márgenes,
viajando de un lugar liminal a otro,
cruzando fronteras en busca del centro.

Es una oración para aquellos cuyo nacimiento
es el paso de oscuridad a oscuridad,
aquellos que se sienten atraídos por la luz,
y avanzan hacia ella,

y para aquellos cuyas jornadas son un camino sinuoso
que comienza y termina en el mismo lugar,
aunque solo al terminar
sabrán por fin donde están.

Para todos los viajeros, jóvenes y viejos,
dolientes y alegres,
cansados y llenos de vida;
los presentes y los ausentes,
los que son como tú (y todos son como tú)
y los que son distintos
(porque de alguna manera todos viajamos solos).

Esta es una oración por la misericordia,
para que andes con pie firme,
y visión clara;
por el pan
para tu cuerpo y tu espíritu,
por el agua;
para que llegues seguro,
y para todos aquellos que encuentres en el camino.

Angela Herrera

# God of the Journey

God of the journey,
may you be both
traveling companion
and mountain guide
on this, our daily walk;
lest unprepared
or ill-equipped
our feet should stumble
on uneven ground,
or clouds obscure
the destination
that we so long to see.

John Birch

# Dios del viaje

Dios del viaje
que seas a la vez
compañero de viaje
y guía de montaña
en este, nuestro camino diario;
para que, mal preparados
o mal equipados,
ni tropiecen nuestros pies
en terreno irregular,
ni oscurezcan las nubes
el destino
que tanto anhelamos ver.

John Birch

The remaining material in this chapter
is presented first in its original Spanish.

# Padrenuestro del peregrino

Padre Nuestro que estás en los caminos,
venga a nosotros Tu aliento
y vela por nosotros los peregrinos;

hágase Tu voluntad
así en el calor como en el frío.

La ruta nuestra de cada día, ilumínala hoy.
Auxilia nuestros desfallecimientos,
así como nosotros auxiliamos a los que desfallecen.

No nos dejes caer en la aflicción
y líbranos de todo mal.

Amén

Autor desconocido


# Pilgrim's Our Father

Our Father who art on the pathway,
ongoing be thy encouragement.

Thy pilgrim watch be known,
Thy will be done
in the heat as it is in the cold.

Enlighten this day our daily route
and help us through our collapses,
as we help those who collapse around us.

And lead us not into distress
but deliver us from evil.

Amen

Author unknown

# Guíame Tú

Jesús, amigo y hermano mío,
Tú que eres camino y luz,
guía mis pasos al caminar.

Abre mis ojos a la vida,
para que sienta en todas las cosas que Tú me amas.

No es fácil ser persona.
A veces, no sé quién soy
ni lo que quiero ser.
Y, sin embargo, desde mi libertad,
anhelo andar por mi pie.
¡Guía, Tú, mis pasos al caminar!

Sé que no he nacido para estar triste;
sé que es mucho lo que me falta por andar;
sé que no hay camino;
sé que soy un bello proyecto.
¡Guía, Tú, mis pasos para llegar a ser yo mismo!

Dame un corazón como el Tuyo,
alegre y generoso.
Dame una voluntad como la Tuya,
capaz de quebrar la rutina.
¡Enséñame a vivir!

Gracias por todos los talentos, gracias por la vida,
gracias por la libertad y el riesgo,
gracias, sobre todo, por Tu amistad.

Jesús, amigo y hermano mío,
guía, Tú, mis pasos hacia la vida,
que es la gran puerta por abrir.

Autor desconocido

# Guide Me

Jesus, my friend and brother,
You who are the way and the light,
guide my steps as I wander.

Open my eyes to life,
so that in all things I feel how much You love me.

It's not easy to be human.
Sometimes, I don't know who I am
or what I want to be.
And, nevertheless, in my freedom,
I long to walk on my own.
Guide my steps as I wander!

I know I was not born to be sad;
I know I still have a long way to walk;
I know there's no set path;
I know I'm quite a project.
Guide my steps as I become myself!

Give me a heart like Yours,
happy and generous.
Give me willpower like Yours,
able to break with routine.
Teach me how to live!

Thank You for all of my talents, thank You for life,
thank You for the freedom to take risks,
thank You, above all, for Your friendship.

Jesus, my friend and brother,
guide my steps toward life,
which is the great door about to open.

Author unknown

# Oración del migrante

Viajar hacia Ti Señor, eso es vivir,
Partir es un poco morir,
Llegar nunca es llegar definitivo hasta descansar en Ti.

Tú, Señor, conociste la migrancia,
Y la hiciste presente a todo hombre
    que comprende qué es vivir,
Y quiere llegar seguro al puerto de la vida.

Tú sacaste de su tierra a Abraham,
    padre de todos los creyentes.
Tú recordaste cuáles eran los caminos para llegar a Ti,
Por los profetas y los apóstoles

Tú mismo te hiciste Migrante del cielo a la tierra,
En el seno de Tu Madre apenas concebido,
En Tu precipitada fuga a Egipto,
Por los caminos sembrando el Evangelio,
Multiplicando el pan, sanando los enfermos,
Y regresando al Padre en Tu ascensión.

Concédenos fe inconmovible,
Esperanza confiada y alegre,
Caridad ardiente y generosa,
Para emigrar con paz en el alma
Y llegar hasta Tí cada día y el último día.

Amen.

Francisco Valdés Subercaseaux

## Migrant's Prayer

The journey towards You, Lord, is life.
To start off is to die a little.
Arrival is never definitive arrival until resting in You.

You, Lord, experienced migrancy.
You made it part of all people
     who know what it is to live
And want to arrive safely at the gates of life.

Out of his land You brought Abraham,
     parent of all believers.
You reminded us which were the paths that lead to You,
Through the prophets and the apostles.

You Yourself became a Migrant from heaven to earth,
As You were conceived in Your mother's womb,
In Your hasty flight to Egypt,
Sowing the Gospel along the roads,
Multiplying bread, healing the sick,
And returning to the Father in Your ascension.

Grant us unshakable faith,
Confident and joyful hope,
Ardent and generous charity,
To emigrate with peace in our souls
And come to You every day and on the last day.

Amen.

Francisco Valdés Subercaseaux

## Credo del Dios peregrino

Creemos en un Dios peregrino,
que sobrepasa fronteras, límites y barreras,
que deja atrás su grandeza y nos encuentra en el camino
y se nos presenta tendiéndonos su mano:
— yo soy el Señor, tu Dios, yo te cuido, voy contigo. —

Creemos en Jesucristo, que caminó nuestra tierra,
que nació fuera de un hogar, que no encontró un lugar,
caminante y peregrino, ya perseguido de niño,
que reveló la justicia y trajo paz a la gente,
que se jugó la vida hasta la misma muerte.

Creemos en el Espíritu, que nos pule
y nos revela con viento fuerte y arena,
y que nos da valor para ser testimonio
de la inmensa gracia de Dios.

Margarita Ouwerkerk

## Creed of the Pilgrim God

We believe in a pilgrim God,
who goes beyond frontiers, limits, and barriers,
who leaves Their greatness behind and meets us on the way
and extends Their hand with this introduction:
"I am the Lord, your God, I'll care for you, I'm going with you."

We believe in Jesus, who walked our earth,
who was born homeless, who found no room,
wanderer and pilgrim, already persecuted as a child,
who revealed justice and brought us peace,
who risked His life until death itself.

We believe in the Spirit, who polishes us
and reveals us with strong winds and sand,
and who sends us the courage to give witness
to the boundless grace of God.

Margarita Ouwerkerk

# Special Places

Sometimes you find yourself in the middle of nowhere.
And sometimes in the middle of nowhere
you find yourself.

(Hummer ad)

*A veces te encuentras en el medio de la nada.*
*Y a veces en el medio de la nada*
*te encuentras.*

# Bendición del peregrino

Oh Dios, que sacaste a Tu siervo Abraham de la ciudad de Ur de los Caldeos, guardándolo en todas sus peregrinaciones, y que fuiste el guía del Pueblo hebreo a través del desierto, Te pedimos que dignes guardar a estos siervos Tuyos que, por amor de Tu Nombre, peregrinan a Compostela.

Sé para ellos compañero en la marcha,
    guía en las encrucijadas,
    aliento en el cansancio,
    defensa en los peligros,
    albergue en el camino,
    abrigo en el frío,
    sombra en el calor,
    luz en la oscuridad,
    consuelo en sus desalientos,
    y firmeza en sus propósitos;

para que, por Tu guía, lleguen incólumes al término de su camino y, enriquecidos de gracias y virtudes, vuelvan ilesos a sus casas, llenos de saludable y perenne alegría.

Por Jesucristo, nuestro Señor, Amén.

Oración del siglo XI

The material in this chapter is presented in geographical order, from East to West, with the original language printed first.

# Pilgrim's Blessing

O God, You led Your servant Abraham out the Chaldean city of Ur, protecting him on all his pilgrimages, and You guided the Hebrew people across the desert. We ask that You deign to watch over these servants of Yours who, for the love of Your Name, are on a pilgrimage to Santiago.

Be their companion in walking,
    wayfinder at crossroads,
    second wind in weariness,
    defense from danger,
    lodging on the path,
    cover in the cold,
    shade from the heat,
    light in the darkness,
    consolation in their sadness,
    and firmness in their purpose.

With Your guidance may they arrive unscathed at the end of the path and, enriched with grace and virtue, may they return unharmed to their homes, filled with healthy and continual joy.

Through Jesus Christ, our Lord, Amen.

11<sup>th</sup> century prayer

## At the Iron Cross

Lord, at the foot of the cross I toss a symbol
of my struggle on this pilgrimage.

On the day when the actions of my life are judged,
may the weight of this stone
help to tip the balance
in favor of my good deeds.

So be it. Amen.

Traditional

## En la Cruz de Ferro

Señor, al pie de la cruz arrojo un símbolo
del esfuerzo de mi peregrinación.

El día en que se juzguen los actos de mi vida,
que el peso de esta piedra
ayude a inclinar la balanza
a favor de mis buenas obras.

Así sea. Amén.

Tradicional

## Oración de La Faba

Aunque hubiera recorrido todos los caminos,
cruzado montañas y valles desde Oriente hasta Occidente,
si no he descubierto la libertad de ser yo mismo
no he llegado a ningún sitio.

Aunque hubiera compartido todos mis bienes
con gentes de otra lengua y cultura,
hecho amistad con peregrinos de mil senderos
o compartido albergue con santos y príncipes,
si no soy capaz de perdonar mañana a mi vecino
no he llegado a ningún sitio.

Aunque hubiera cargado mi mochila de principio a fin
y esperado por cada peregrino necesitado de ánimo,
o cedido mi cama a quien llegó después
y regalado mi botellín de agua a cambio de nada,
si de regreso a mi casa y mi trabajo no soy capaz
de crear fraternidad y poner alegría, paz y unidad,
no he llegado a ningún sitio.

Aunque hubiera tenido comida y agua cada día
y disfrutado de techo y ducha todas las noches
o hubiera sido bien atendido de mis heridas,
si no he descubierto en todo ello el amor de Dios,
no he llegado a ningún sitio.

Aunque hubiera visto todos los monumentos
y contemplado las mejores puestas de sol;
Aunque hubiera aprendido un saludo en cada idioma,
o probado el agua limpia de todas las fuentes,
si no he descubierto quién es autor
de tanta belleza gratuita y de tanta paz
no he llegado a ningún sitio.

Si a partir de hoy no sigo caminando en tus caminos,
buscando y viviendo según lo aprendido;
Si a partir de hoy no veo en cada persona,
amigo y enemigo, un compañero de camino;
Si a partir de hoy no reconozco a Dios,
el Dios de Jesús de Nazaret,
como el único Dios de mi vida,
no he llegado a ningún sitio

FrayDino

## La Faba Prayer

Though I travel all the paths,
crossing mountains and valleys from East to West,
if I don't find the freedom to be myself
I have arrived nowhere.

Though I share all my possessions
with people of other languages and cultures,
make friends with pilgrims on a thousand paths
or share lodging with saints and princes;
if I'm unable to forgive my neighbor tomorrow
I have arrived nowhere.

Though I carry my pack from beginning to end
and provide encouragement to every pilgrim who needs it,
or turn over my bed to someone who arrives after me
and give away my water bottle in exchange for nothing;
if I go home and am unable to promote unity where I live
or spread peace and happiness where I work,
I have arrived nowhere.

Though I have food and water each day
and enjoy a roof and shower every night
or have my injuries treated well;
if I don't discover the love of God in those things,
I have arrived nowhere.

Though I see all the historic monuments
and witness the most amazing sunsets;
though I learn a greeting in every language
and drink clean water from every fountain;
if I don't discover who is the author
of all this free beauty and peace,
I have arrived nowhere.

Starting today, if I don't continue walking in your ways,
searching and living according to what I have learned;
starting today, if I can't see every person,
friend or foe. as a companion on my path;
starting today, if I don't recognize God,
the God of Jesus of Nazareth,
as the only God of my life,
I have arrived nowhere.

FrayDino

# Peregrinos a Santiago

Polvo, barro, sol y lluvia
es Camino de Santiago.
Millares de peregrinos
y más de un millar de años.

Peregrino ¿Quién te llama?
¿Qué fuerza oculta te atrae?
Ni el campo de las Estrellas
ni las grandes catedrales.

No es la bravura Navarra,
ni el vino de los riojanos
ni los mariscos gallegos,
ni los campos castellanos.

Peregrino ¿Quién te llama?
¿Qué fuerza oculta te atrae?
Ni las gentes del Camino
ni las costumbres rurales.

No es la historia y la cultura,
ni el gallo de la Calzada
ni el palacio de Gaudí,
ni el castillo Ponferrada.

Todo lo veo al pasar,
y es un gozo verlo todo,
mas la voz que a mí me llama
la siento mucho más hondo.

La fuerza que a mí me empuja
la fuerza que a mí me atrae,
no sé explicarla ni yo.
¡Solo El de arriba lo sabe!

Eugenio Garibay Baños

# Pilgrims to Santiago

Dust, mud, sun and rain
is the Camino de Santiago.
Thousands of pilgrims
and more than a thousand years.

Pilgrim, who calls you?
What hidden force attracts you?
Neither the field of stars
nor the great cathedrals.

It's not Navarran bravery,
nor the wine of the Riojans
nor Galician seafood,
nor Castilian fields.

Pilgrim, who calls you?
What hidden force attracts you?
Neither the people of the Camino
nor the rural customs.

It's not history and culture,
nor the rooster of La Calzada
nor Gaudi's palace,
nor Ponferrada castle.

I see everything as it passes by,
and it's a joy to see all of it,
but the voice that calls me
I feel much more deeply.

The force that pushes me,
the force that attracts me,
even I don't know how to explain it.
Only the one above knows!

Eugenio Garibay Baños

# Finisterre

At the Western edge of the world
We pray for our sins to fall from us
As chains from the limbs of penitents.

We have walked out of the lives we had
And will return to nothing, if we live,
Changed by the journey, face and soul alike.

We have walked out of our lives
To come to where the walls of heaven
Are thin as a curtain, transparent as glass,

Where the Apostle spoke the holy words,
Where in death he returned, where God is close,
Where saints and martyrs mark the road.

Santiago, *primus ex apostolis*,
Defender of pilgrims, warrior for truth,
Take from our backs the burdens of this life,

What we have done, who we have been;
Take them as fire takes the cloth
They cast into the sea at Finisterre.

Robert Dickinson

# Finisterre

En el extremo occidental del mundo
Rogamos que nuestros pecados se desprendan de nosotros
Como cadenas de las extremidades de penitentes.

Hemos salido caminando de las vidas que teníamos
Y regresaremos a la nada, si vivimos,
Cambiados por el viaje, la cara y el alma por igual.

Hemos salido de nuestras vidas
Para venir donde las murallas del cielo
Son delgadas como una cortina, transparentes como el cristal,

Donde el apóstol decía las palabras sagradas,
Adonde en la muerte regresó, donde Dios está cerca,
Donde santos y mártires señalan el camino.

Santiago, *primus ex apostolis*,
Defensor de los peregrinos, guerrero por la verdad,
Quita de nuestras espaldas las cargas de esta vida,

Lo que hemos hecho, quienes hemos sido;
Quítalo como el fuego quema la tela
Que se arroja al mar en Finisterre.

Robert Dickinson

# Song Lyrics

Who am I in this frightened world?
Where will I make my bed tonight
when twilight turns to dark?

(Paul Simon)


*¿Quién soy yo en este mundo asustado?*
*¿Dónde haré la cama esta noche*
*cuando el crepúsculo se vuelva oscuro?*

# Le chant des pèlerins de Compostelle (Ultreïa)

Tous les matins, nous prenons le chemin,
tous les matins, nous allons plus loin,
jour après jour, la route nous appelle,
c'est la voix de Compostelle.

*Ultreïa! Ultreïa! Et sus eïa!*
*Deus, adjuva nos!*

Chemin de terre et chemin de Foi,
voie millénaire de l'Europe,
la Voie lactée de Charlemagne,
c'est le chemin de tous les jacquets.

*Ultreïa! Ultreïa! Et sus eïa!*
*Deus, adjuva nos!*

Et tout là-bas au bout du continent,
messire Jacques nous attend,
depuis toujours son sourire fixe
le soleil qui meurt au Finisterre.

*Ultreïa! Ultreïa! Et sus eïa!*
*Deus, adjuva nos!*

Jean-claude Benazet

## Song of the Pilgrims of Compostela (Ultreya)

Every morning we take to the road,
every morning we go further on,
day after day, the route is calling to us,
it's the voice of Compostela.

A path of dirt and a path made of faith,
crossing Europe for a thousand years,
the Milky Way of Charlemagne,
is the path of pilgrims to St. James.

And way out at the continent's end,
noble Santiago is waiting for us,
in a smile that never fails to appear
as the sunset ends in Finisterre.

Jean-claude Benazet
*Translation by GC Clark approved by JC Benazet*


## La canción de los peregrinos de Compostela (Ultreia)

Cada mañana, a caminar,
cada mañana, más allá,
día tras día, la meta nos llama,
es la voz de Compostela.

Senda de tierra, senda de fe,
vía milenaria de Europa,
la Vía láctea de Carlomagno
es el camino jacobeo.

Y al final del continente
Sant Yago nos espera ya,
y veremos su eterna sonrisa
al caer el sol sobre la mar,

Jean-claude Benazet
*Translatied by JC Benazet and José María Maldonado*

# The Road to Santiago

A townsman's life is even,
 like the dust upon the road;
Not changing with the seasons —
 just fortune's fickle load.
But sitting on my step and
 bending hide and thread to task,
I saw the first man walking,
 I saw the first man walking,
 I saw the first of many walking past.

In ones and twos they traveled;
 the first hints of the wave.
With hat and stick and scallop
 they would go to see the grave
Of the Saint who'd lived among us,
 a town he'd come to save
As he walked along the road to Santiago.

With pennies in their pockets
 and blisters on their feet,
They'd come within their weariness,
 the humble and the meek,
For while a day could bring them wages,
 these months would bring release
From the road that they were walking,
 This road that they were walking,
 This road that led them forth in their belief.

Soon the trickle was a torrent;
    then the torrent was a flood.
And like Noah, how they laughed
    amid the gadflies and the mud.
And I wondered what they shared
    that made such disparate men beloved
As they walked along the road to Santiago?

For one had come from Germany,
    and one from here in Spain,
And one from near the Bosporus
    where Constantine had reigned.
From every land they sallied forth,
    then ventured home again,
And found a road worth walking,
    They found this road worth walking,
    For all agreed their roads were much the same.

And so I laid my work aside —
    the day's long toils would keep,
For, what was said? "A man must sow
    if he intends to reap."
So, with a laugh,
    I set to putting blisters on my feet
As I joined them on the road to Santiago.

Heather Dale

# Pilgrim

There is a heavenly city
That I'm compelled to find,
Though I love the flowers and trees
And the smell of the grinding seed
And all the beautiful things here in life.

I'm a pilgrim here
On this side of the great divide.
I'm a pilgrim here,
But I'll walk with you for a while.

Nobody's ever quite ready
But they all take the ride.
Many have died with the promise inside
They never got to see it in their time.

I'm a pilgrim here
On this side of the great divide.
I'm a pilgrim here,
But I'll walk with you for a while.
I'll hold you for a while.
I'll love you here for a while.

John Mark McMillan

# Peregrino

Hay una ciudad celestial
Que me veo impelido a encontrar,
Aunque amo las flores y los árboles
Y el olor de la molienda de semillas
Y todas las cosas bellas de la vida.

Yo aquí soy peregrino
En este lado de la gran divisoria.
Yo aquí soy peregrino
Pero caminaré contigo un rato.

Nadie está nunca muy preparado
Pero todos hacen el viaje.
Muchos murieron con la promesa dentro
Nunca llegaron a verla en sus tiempos.

Yo aquí soy peregrino
En este lado de la gran divisoria.
Yo aquí soy peregrino
Pero caminaré contigo un rato.
Te abrazaré un rato.
Te amaré aquí un rato.

John Mark McMillan

# Santiago

We have walked here for a thousand years.
Shoes have worn away the stone
And my bootprints in the Spanish dirt
They will be here when I'm gone.

All of our paths join on this single road.
The sign of the seashell shows the way.
We all have our reasons why we started out,
But the end of our journey is the same.

Santiago was a fisherman.
Made his living from the sea
'Til he met up with a traveler
Who said, "Come along with me."

The nets he carefully mended there,
He dropped them and he walked away.
And now we meet on this dusty road
That leads down to the salty spray: The Way.

I may get to hike a thousand miles
But my time will come to pass
When all these rocks give way to endlessness
And the ocean waves will crash.

I'll follow these arrows to the setting sun.
The blazes are yellow, so I know.
There will be darkness when the day is done
So I'll walk in the sunlight as I go.

I will live my life like it's no mistake,
Carry everything I need,
Take the steps that are left to take,
And follow where the blazes lead.

Every pilgrim that has passed by here
Left a trail that I can trust.
I know most of me will disappear
Like my bootprints in the dust.

David Wilcox

# The Wayfaring Pilgrim

I am a poor wayfaring pilgrim,
Wandering through this world below.
But there's no sickness, toil nor danger
In that bright world to which I go.
I'm going there to see my father,
I'm going there no more to roam.
I'm just a-going over Jordan,
I'm just a-going over home.

I know dark clouds will gather over me,
I know my pathway's rough and steep;
But golden fields lie there before me,
And weary eyes no more shall weep.
I'm going there to see my mother,
She said she'd meet me when I come.
I'm just a-going over Jordan,
I'm just a-going over home.

I'll soon be free from every trial,
My body sleeping in the sod;
I'll drop the cross of self-denial,
And enter to my great reward.
I'm going there to see my Savior,
And sing God's praise forevermore.
I'm just a-going over Jordan,
I'm just a-going to that shore.

American folk song

# Poetry

The stars began to burn through the sheets of clouds,
and there was a new voice
which you slowly recognized as your own.

(Mary Oliver)

*Las estrellas comenzaron a quemar las capas de nubes,*
*y hubo una nueva voz*
*que poco a poco reconociste como la tuya.*

# The Road Not Taken

Two roads diverged in a yellow wood,
And sorry I could not travel both
And be one traveler, long I stood
And looked down one as far as I could
To where it bent in the undergrowth;

Then took the other, as just as fair,
And having perhaps the better claim,
Because it was grassy and wanted wear;
Though as for that the passing there
Had worn them really about the same,

And both that morning equally lay
In leaves no step had trodden black.
Oh, I kept the first for another day!
Yet knowing how way leads on to way,
I doubted if I should ever come back.

I shall be telling this with a sigh
Somewhere ages and ages hence:
Two roads diverged in a wood, and I —
I took the one less traveled by,
And that has made all the difference.

Robert Frost

# El camino no tomado

Dos caminos se bifurcaban en un bosque amarillo,
Y apenado por no poder tomar ambos
Y ser un viajero solo, me detuve largo rato
Y miré uno de ellos tan lejos como pude
Hasta donde giraba en la espesura;

Tomé entonces el otro, igual de hermoso,
Y siendo quizá el más atrayente,
Pues era tupido y quería pisadas;
Aunque en realidad allí el trasiego
De hecho los había desgastado por igual,

Y esa mañana a los dos de la misma forma
Cubrían hojas sin huella de haber sido pisadas.
¡Oh, dejé el primero para otro día!
Aun sabiendo como un camino lleva a otro,
Dudé que alguna vez fuera a regresar.

Estaré contando esto con un suspiro
En algún lugar en el futuro, así pasen muchos años:
Dos caminos se bifurcaban en un bosque, y yo —
Yo tomé el menos transitado,
Y eso ha marcado la diferencia.

Robert Frost

# Song of the Open Road, 1

Afoot and light-hearted I take to the open road,
Healthy, free, the world before me,
The long brown path before me leading wherever I choose.

Henceforth I ask not good-fortune,
I myself am good-fortune,
Henceforth I whimper no more,
    postpone no more, need nothing,
Done with indoor complaints, libraries, querulous criticisms,
Strong and content I travel the open road.

The earth, that is sufficient,
I do not want the constellations any nearer,
I know they are very well where they are,
I know they suffice for those who belong to them.

(Still here I carry my old delicious burdens,
I carry them, men and women,
I carry them with me wherever I go,
I swear it is impossible for me to get rid of them,
I am fill'd with them, and I will fill them in return.)

Walt Whitman

# Canción del camino abierto, 1

A pie y con el corazón tranquilo, tomo el camino abierto,
Saludable, libre, el mundo se abre ante mi,
La larga ruta parda ante mi orientándome adonde yo elija.

A partir de ahora no pido buena fortuna,
Yo mismo soy buena fortuna,
A partir de ahora no me quejo más,
    no pospongo más, nada necesito,
Harto de lamentos interiores, bibliotecas, críticas molestas,
Poderoso y contento recorro el camino abierto.

La tierra, con eso basta,
No quiero las constelaciones más cerca,
Sé que están muy bien allí donde están,
Sé que son suficiente para aquellos que les pertenecen.

(Aquí todavía llevo mis viejas y deliciosas cargas,
Las llevo, hombres y mujeres,
Las llevo conmigo adonde quiera que vaya,
Juro que me es imposible deshacerme de ellas,
Estoy lleno de ellas y, a cambio, las haré plenas.)

Walt Whitman

## It's a Question of Prayer

Monks know we can be one

with what has no
words, no name, not even a murmur.

There we meet the modesty
of presence: It could be green,

slow, tattered, cold, alone
as a possum

crossing a backroad.
It's the touch

of the still. Prayer
is a place where we are

always
allowed in.

We are Amen, Shalom, Namaste.

Our where, there, here,
our forgotten habitat of yes.

We become sigh, our "I"
the wisteria vine in the rain,

the wet dog,
the house sparrow

nesting in the stillness of brown.

Jack Ridl

# Es una cuestión de oración

Los monjes saben que podemos ser uno

con lo que no tiene
palabras, ni nombre, ni siquiera un murmullo.

Allí nos encontramos con la modestia
de presencia: podría ser verde,

lento, harapiento, frío, solo
como una zarigüeya

cruzando una carretera secundaria.
Es el toque

de la calma. Oración
es un lugar donde

siempre
somos admitidos.

Somos Amen, Shalom, Namasté.

Nuestro donde, allí, aquí,
nuestro olvidado hábitat del sí.

Nos convertimos en suspiro, nuestro «yo»
la flor de glicina bajo la lluvia,

el perro mojado,
el gorrión

anidando en la quietud del marrón.

Jack Ridl

# The Bridge Builder

An old man going a lone highway,
Came, at the evening cold and gray,
To a chasm vast and deep and wide.
Through which was flowing a sullen tide

The old man crossed in the twilight dim,
The sullen stream had no fear for him;
But he turned when safe on the other side
And built a bridge to span the tide.

"Old man," said a fellow pilgrim near,
"You are wasting your strength with building here;
Your journey will end with the ending day,
You never again will pass this way;
You've crossed the chasm, deep and wide,
Why build this bridge at evening tide?"

The builder lifted his old gray head;
"Good friend, in the path I have come," he said,
"There followed after me to-day
A youth whose feet must pass this way.
This chasm that has been as naught to me
To that fair-haired youth may a pitfall be.
He, too, must cross in the twilight dim;
Good friend, I am building this bridge for him!"

Will Allen Dromgoole

# El constructor de puentes

Caminaba un anciano por un sendero desolado,
al caer la tarde de un día frío y nublado.
Llegó él a un barranco muy ancho y escabroso
por cuyo fondo corría un lúgubre arroyo.

Cruzó así al otro lado en la tenue luz del día,
pues aquello al anciano ningún miedo ofrecía.
Al llegar a la otra orilla construyó el hombre un puente
que hiciera más seguro atravesar la corriente.

— ¡Escuche! —, le dijo un viajero que pasaba por allí,
— malgasta usted su tiempo al construir un puente aquí.
Su viaje ya termina, pues ha llegado el fin del día
y ya nunca más transitará por esta vía.
Ha cruzado el barranco, dejando atrás lo más duro,
¿por qué construye un puente, estando ya tan oscuro? —

El anciano constructor levantó entonces la cabeza:
— Es que por este mismo camino — , respondió con firmeza,
— noté que hace algunas horas me trataba de alcanzar
un jovencito inexperto que por acá ha de cruzar.
Este profundo barranco para mí no ha sido nada,
mas para el joven que viene será una encrucijada.
En las sombras pasará cuando llegue aquí,
es por eso que para él este puente construí — .

Will Allen Dromgoole
(translator unknown)

---

The remaining poetry is presented first in its original Spanish.

# Peregrino

¿Volver? Vuelva el que tenga,
Tras largos años, tras un largo viaje,
Cansancio del camino y la codicia
De su tierra, su casa, sus amigos,
Del amor que al regreso fiel le espere.

Mas, ¿tú? ¿Volver? Regresar no piensas,
Sino seguir libre adelante,
Disponible por siempre, mozo o viejo,
Sin hijo que te busque, como a Ulises,
Sin Ítaca que aguarde y sin Penélope.

Sigue, sigue adelante y no regreses,
Fiel hasta el fin del camino y tu vida,
No eches de menos un destino más fácil,
Tus pies sobre la tierra antes no hollada,
Tus ojos frente a lo antes nunca visto.

Luis Cernuda

# Pilgrim

Return? Let them return who are,
After long years, after a long journey,
Tired of the road and the burning desire
For their land, their home, their friends,
For the faithful love expecting their return.

But you? Return? You don't plan to turn back,
Rather to go forward free,
Unattached forever, youth or elder,
Without a child searching for you, like Ulysses,
Without Ithaca waiting and without Penelope.

Go on, keep going forward and don't go back,
Faithful to the end of the road and your life,
Don't long for an easier destination,
Your feet on a land not found before,
Your eyes facing what's never been seen.

Luis Cernuda

# Santiago: Balada ingenua

25 Julio 1918, Fuente Vaqueros, Granada

I

Esta noche ha pasado Santiago
su camino de luz en el cielo.
Lo comentan los niños jugando
con el agua de un cauce sereno.

¿Dónde va el peregrino celeste
por el claro infinito sendero?
Va a la aurora que brilla en el fondo
en caballo blanco como el hielo.

¡Niños chicos, cantad en el prado
horadando con risas al viento!

Dice un hombre que ha visto a Santiago
en tropel con doscientos guerreros;
iban todos cubiertos de luces,
con guirnaldas de verdes luceros,
y el caballo que monta Santiago
era un astro de brillos intensos.

Dice el hombre que cuenta la historia
que en la noche dormida se oyeron
tremolar plateado de alas
que en sus ondas llevose el silencio.

¿Qué sería que el río parose?
Eran ángeles los caballeros.

¡Niños chicos, cantad en el prado
horadando con risas al viento!

Es la noche de luna menguante.
¡Escuchad! ¿Qué se siente en el cielo,
que los grillos refuerzan sus cuerdas
y dan voces los perros vegueros?

# Saint James: Naïve Ballad

July 25, 1918, Fuente Vaqueros, Granada

I

Tonight Saint James travelled
his path of light in the heavens.
The children discuss this, playing
with the water of a calm riverbed.

Where is the celestial pilgrim going
on the infinite clear path?
He's going to the dawn that shines in the distance
on a horse as white as ice.

Little children, sing in the field
piercing the wind with laughter!

A man says he has seen Saint James
in a host of two hundred warriors;
they were all covered in lights
with garlands of green stars
and the horse Saint James was riding
was a star of intense brightness.

The man who tells the story says
that in the sleeping night was heard
the silvery flutter of wings
which the silence carried off on its waves.

What could have made the river stop flowing?
The knights were angels.

Little children, sing in the field
piercing the wind with laughter!

It's the night of the waning moon.
Listen! What do they sense in the heavens,
that crickets strengthen their strings
and the meadow dogs cry out?

*(Santiago: Balada ingenua)*

— Madre abuela, ¿cuál es el camino,
madre abuela, que yo no lo veo?

— Mira bien y verás una cinta
de polvillo harinoso y espeso,
un borrón que parece de plata
o de nácar. ¿Lo ves?
— Ya lo veo.

— Madre abuela. ¿Dónde está Santiago?
— Por allí marcha con su cortejo,
la cabeza llena de plumajes
y de perlas muy finas el cuerpo,
con la luna rendida a sus plantas,
con el sol escondido en el pecho.

Esta noche en la vega se escuchan
los relatos brumosos del cuento.

¡Niños chicos, cantad en el prado,
horadando con risas al viento!

II

Una vieja que vive muy pobre
en la parte más alta del pueblo,
que posee una rueca inservible,
una virgen y dos gatos negros,
mientras hace la ruda calceta
con sus secos y temblones dedos,
rodeada de buenas comadres
y de sucios chiquillos traviesos,
en la paz de la noche tranquila,
con las sierras perdidas en negro,
va contando con ritmos tardíos
la visión que ella tuvo en sus tiempos.

*(St. James: Naïve Ballad)*

"Grandmother, which is the path,
grandmother, since I can't see it?"

"Look carefully and you'll see a ribbon
of powder, floury and thick,
a smudge that looks like it's made of silver
or mother of pearl. Do you see it?"
"Now I do. "

"Grandmother, where is Saint James?"
"He's out there marching with his cortege,
his head covered in plumage
and his body in very fine pearls,
with the moon yielding at his feet,
with the sun hidden in his chest."

Tonight in the meadow you can hear
the misty accounts of the story.

Little children, sing in the field
piercing the wind with laughter!

II

An old lady who lives very humbly
in the highest part of the village,
who owns a useless spinning wheel,
an image of the virgin and two black cats,
while she does rough knitting
with her dry and shaky fingers,
surrounded by good friends
and dirty little mischievous children,
in the peace of the tranquil night,
with the mountains lost in blackness,
she relates at a slow pace
the vision she had in her time.

*(Santiago: Balada ingenua)*

Ella vio en una noche lejana
como ésta, sin ruidos ni vientos,
el apóstol Santiago en persona,
peregrino en la tierra del cielo.

— Y comadre, ¿cómo iba vestido?
— la preguntan dos voces a un tiempo. —

— Con bordón de esmeraldas y perlas
y una túnica de terciopelo.

Cuando hubo pasado la puerta,
mis palomas sus alas tendieron,
y mi perro, que estaba dormido,
fue tras él sus pisadas lamiendo.

Era dulce el Apóstol divino,
más aún que la luna de enero.
A su paso dejó por la senda
un olor de azucena y de incienso.

— Y comadre, ¿no le dijo nada?
— la preguntan dos voces a un tiempo. —

— Al pasar me miró sonriente
y una estrella dejome aquí dentro.

— ¿Dónde tienes guardada esa estrella?
— la pregunta un chiquillo travieso. —

— ¿Se ha apagado — dijéronle otros —
como cosa de un encantamiento?
— No, hijos míos, la estrella relumbra,
que en el alma clavada la llevo.

— ¿Cómo son las estrellas aquí?
— Hijo mío, igual que en el cielo.

*(St. James: Naïve Ballad)*

She saw, on a night long ago
like this one, without noise or wind,
the apostle Saint James in person,
pilgrim in the land of heaven.

"And neighbor, how was he dressed?"
two voices ask her at the same time.

"With a pilgrim staff of emeralds and pearls
and a tunic of velvet.

"When he had passed the door,
my doves stretched their wings,
and my dog, who was asleep,
went after him, licking his footsteps.

"The divine Apostle was sweet,
even more than the January moon.
As he passed down the path he left behind
a fragrance of lilies and incense."

"And neighbor, didn't he say anything to you?"
two voices ask her at the same time.

"As he passed he looked at me smiling
and left a star here inside me."

"Where do you keep that star?"
a mischievous child asks her.

"Has it gone out," others asked her
"like something from an enchantment?"
"No, my children, the star is dazzling,
I carry it embedded in my soul."

"What are stars like here?"
"My son, the same as in the heavens."

*(Santiago: Balada ingenua)*

— Siga, siga la vieja comadre.
¿Dónde iba el glorioso viajero?

— Se perdió por aquellas montañas
con mis blancas palomas y el perro.
Pero llena dejome la casa
de rosales y de jazmineros,
y las uvas verdes en la parra
maduraron, y mi troje lleno
encontré la siguiente mañana.
Todo obra del Apóstol bueno.

— ¡Grande suerte que tuvo, comadre!
— sermonean dos voces a un tiempo. —

Los chiquillos están ya dormidos
y los campos en hondo silencio.

¡Niños chicos, pensad en Santiago
por los turbios caminos del sueño!

¡Noche clara, finales de julio!
¡Ha pasado Santiago en el cielo!

La tristeza que tiene mi alma,
por el blanco camino la dejo,
para ver si la encuentran los niños
y en el agua la vayan hundiendo,
para ver si en la noche estrellada
a muy lejos la llevan los vientos.

Federico García Lorca

*(St. James: Naïve Ballad)*

"Continue, continue old friend.
Where was the glorious traveler headed?"

"He lost himself in those mountains
with my white doves and the dog.
But he left my house full
of roses and jasmine bushes,
and the green grapes on the vine
ripened, and I found my barn
full the next morning.
All the doing of the good Apostle."

"What good luck you had, neighbor!"
two voices preach at the same time.

The children are already asleep
and the fields in deep silence.

Little children, think about Saint James
on the hazy paths of dreams!

Clear night, late July!
Saint James passed by in the heavens!

The sadness I have in my heart
I'll leave behind on the white path,
to see if the children find it
and in the water go drown it,
to see if in the star-filled night
the winds carry it far, far away.

Federico García Lorca

103

# Proverbios y cantares XXIX

Caminante, son tus huellas
el camino, y nada más;
caminante, no hay camino,
se hace camino al andar.
Al andar se hace camino,
y al volver la vista atrás
se ve la senda que nunca
se ha de volver a pisar.
Caminante, no hay camino,
sino estelas en la mar.

Antonio Machado

# Proverbs and Songs 29

Wanderer, your footprints are
the path, and nothing else;
wanderer, there is no path,
the path is made by walking.
Walking makes the path,
and on glancing back
one sees the path
that must never be trod again.
Wanderer, there is no path —
Just your wake in the sea.

Antonio Machado
Translated by Betty Jean Craige

# Afterword

i thank You God for most this amazing day
. . . and for everything which is natural

(e e cummings)

*Te agradezco Dios más este día asombroso
. . . y todo lo que es natural*

# About the author

In college I studied Spanish language, literature, and history. I lived for a year in Madrid and was able to visit the Cathedral in Santiago and see the Apostle's tomb. I also read Michener's *Iberia*, which devotes several pages to the Way of St. James, but the knowledge did not stick. I earned a BA in Spanish from Cornell University (Ithaca, NY, USA) and then an MA in Education from the University of Rochester (NY, USA). I taught high school Spanish for seven years, then changed directions and began helping teachers use technology.

The last eighteen years of my career were spent in the Kaneb Center for Teaching and Learning at the University of Notre Dame (Indiana, USA). I gave workshops and provided consulations. I wrote a successful blog, explored new technologies, and taught a course on multimedia. I was also given the opportunity to spend summer 2009 teaching in Toledo (Spain) and was exposed to the Camino once more. It rocketed to the top of my bucket list and I went home with a *credencial*, map, and guidebook!

I retired to West Michigan in July 2019 and planned to walk the Camino the following Spring. I talked with several people about coming along with me. A local friend got excited but developed knee issues. A Spanish buddy was still working and had kids in college. Then I approached my best friend from high school, who was also retiring. We were inseparable from ages 12 through 18 but forty years later we had not seen much of each other. I thought it was a long shot, but he surprised me with an emphatic "yes!"

From summer through Christmas I obsessed over shoes, packs, and other gear. I made lists and read books. I practiced Spanish by reading and listening to podcasts. I took a three-day hike and raised nearly $2000 for charity. AND I began to collect the material that would evolve into this book. My friend visited after New Year's and we bought plane tickets. Then COVID-19 hit.

On April 2 our tickets were canceled. Along with thousands of other potential pilgrims, we were crushed. I was very fortunate during the pandemic, but it was still challenging. Editing this book was a major consolation. It's only fitting that the project was finished on the feast day of St. James *and* St. Christopher!

— Chris Clark
July 25, 2020

# About Sister Macrina

Sr. Macrina Wiederkehr, O.S.B. was a spiritual guide, retreat facilitator, and author who made her home in the monastic community of St. Scholastica (Fort Smith, Arkansas, USA). She wrote nine books, including *The Circle of Life*, co-authored with Joyce Rupp. Macrina's retreats guided seekers through experiences of silence, contemplation, and faith sharing. She saw God's presence in nature, relationships, and daily activities:

> *My God is not imprisoned anywhere, not in the Bible*
> *nor the tabernacle. Real Presence is everywhere,*
> *and those with the hearts of children revel in it.*

As I began contacting authors for permission I was saddened to learn that Macrina Wiederkehr had died only a few days earlier. We had never met, but I remember being moved by the poetry of "Pilgrim Blessing" (page 32) as I read Joyce Rupp's *Walk in a Relaxed Manner*. Macrina had written it specifically for the book by her friend. On the day I impulsively decided to dedicate this book to Sr. Macrina, a line from her blessing inspired both the title of the book and my own prayer contribution. I have come to believe the dedication decision was providential, rather than impetuous.

# Credits

"**At the Iron Cross**" is based on a popular prayer that pilgrims have used at the Cruz de Ferro.

"**The Backpack of My Soul**" is by **G. Christopher Clark** (b. 1953), a retired educator who lives in Fennville, Michigan, USA.

"**Bendición del peregrino**" (Pilgrim's Blessing) is an 11th-century prayer offered every evening at a mass for pilgrims in Roncesvalles, a small Basque village at the eastern edge of the *Camino Francés*.

"**The Bridge Builder**" is by **Will Allen Dromgoole** (1864-1934), a female journalist and author from Murfreesboro, Tennessee, USA, who published thirteen books, 7500 poems, and 5000 essays. The author of the Spanish translation is unknown.

"**Camino Call**" is a prayer by **Rick Zweck** (1953-2016), who was the Founding Pastor at Pacific Lutheran College in Queensland, Australia. He walked the Camino in 2013 and later used this prayer to introduce people to a labyrinth at the college. The prayer is included with permission.

"**Canticle of the Sun**" is excerpted from *Laudes Creaturarum*, by **St. Francis of Assisi** (1181-1226), an Italian friar and mystic who, legend has it, made the pilgrimage to Santiago in 1214. The Spanish translation of the song is from es.Wikipedia.org

"**Challenge Lover's Prayer**" is by **Rosemerry Wahtola Trommer** (b.1969), a poet from Colorado, USA. The poem appears in her book, *Hush* (Middle Creek Publishing 2020), and is reprinted with permission.

"**Le chant des pèlerins de Compostelle**" (Song of the Compostela Pilgrims) is by **Jean-claude Benazet** (b.1950) of Lavaur, Midi-Pyrenees, France. The song was written in 1989 and the lyrics are reprinted with permission.

"**Credo del Dios peregrino**" (Creed of the Pilgrim God) is a prayer by **Margarita Ouwerkerk** (b. 1965), of Buenos Aires, Argentina. It was composed in 2016 at *Red Crearte* (redcrearte.org.ar), an ecumenical network that develops artistic resources for churches in Latin America. The prayer is included with permission.

"**The Deer's Cry**" is a prayer of protection attributed to **St. Patrick** (386-461). It was set to music on Shaun Davey's album, "The Pilgrim" (Tara Music 1983). The text is from a medieval Irish work, translated by Kuno Meyer. It is included with permission. According to legend, St. Patrick prayed this after being warned of an ambush. When the monks passed by, all that the would-be attackers saw was a herd of deer.

"**Dum Pater Familias**" (When God the Father) comes from the *Codex Calixtinus*, a 12th-century encyclopedia for the pilgrimage and cult of St. James.

"**Father Mychal's Prayer**" was composed by **Mychal Judge** OFM (1933-2001), a Franciscan friar in New York City (USA) who served as chaplain to the fire department and was the first certified fatality of the September 11 attacks. The prayer is included with permission

"**Finisterre**" was written by **Robert Dickinson** (b. 1962), a writer who lives in Brighton, England. The text is an excerpt from the libretto of "Path of Miracles," a 2005 composition by Joby Talbot. It is included with permission.

"**For Those Who Have Far to Travel**" is a blessing by **Jan Richardson**, a Florida (USA) artist, writer, and minister who serves as director of The Wellspring Studio, LLC (janrichardson.com). The blessing appears in *Circle of Grace: A Book of Blessings for the Seasons* (Wanton Gospeller Press, 2015) and is included with permission.

"**God of the Journey**" is a prayer by **John Birch** (b. 1954), a Methodist Local Preacher in Kidwelly, Wales, UK. The prayer first appeared on the "Faith & Worship" website in 2016, and it is included with permission.

"**The Grasp of Your Hand**" is by **Rabindranath Tagore** (1861-1941), a writer and philosopher from Bengal, India. The work is titled "79" in the book *Fruit-Gathering* (Macmillian 1916). The translation comes from a Jesuit website, pastoralsj.org.

"**Great Spirit Prayer**" was translated into English in 1887 by Yellow Lark (b. ca. 1850), a leader of the **Lakota** people of the north-central USA. It was found on the website of the Akta Lakota Museum and Cultural Center, South Dakota, USA.

"**Guíame Tú**" (Guide Me) is a prayer of unknown authorship that first appeared online in 2010.

"**Irish Blessing**" is an English translation of an ancient Celtic prayer.

"**It's a Question of Prayer**" is by **Jack Ridl** (b.1944), a poet who taught at Hope College and now lives in Saugatuck, Michigan, USA. The poem appeared in *Southern Poetry Review* (2016) and subsequently in *Saint Peter and the Goldfinch* (Wayne State U. Press 2019). It is included with permission.

"**Lord, Be a Bright Flame**" is a paraphrase of a prayer credited to **St. Columba**, a 6th-century abbot from Donegal who is called *Colmcille* in Ireland. (this is not St. Columba of Cordoba)

"**May I Walk**" is a prayer by **Robert C. Morris** (b. 1941), an Episcopal priest who directs an interfaith learning community in Summit, New Jersey, USA. It appeared in *Wrestling with Grace* (Upper Room 2003) and is included with permission.

"**Morning and Evening Prayers**" come from **the Boran people** of Ethiopia and Kenya. They appear in Desmond Tutu's *An African Prayer Book* (Walker 1995) but were originally published as early as 1845.

"**A Mountaineer's Prayer**" is by **Lucy Larcom** (1824-1893), a poet and educator from Beverly, Massachusetts, USA. The poem appeared in *Wild Roses of Cape Ann* (Riverside 1881).

"**Nada te turbe**" (Let Nothing Disturb You) is by **St. Teresa of Avila** (1515-1582), a Spanish noblewoman who became a Carmelite nun and theologian. This is the first section of a prayer which the saint is said to have carried as a bookmark in her missal.

"**On the Path to a Holy Well**" is a prayer of unknown authorship. It was found on the website of the Holy Wells of Cork and Kerry (Ireland).

"**Oración de La Faba**" (La Faba Prayer) is a prayer by **FrayDino** (b. 1970), a Franciscan friar in La Coruña, Spain. The prayer was written while the author served at the *albergue* in La Faba, and it is included with permission.

"**Oración del migrante**" (Migrant's Prayer) is an unpublished work by **Francisco Valdés Subercaseaux** (1908-1982), who was the Catholic Bishop of Osorno, Chile.

"**Padrenuestro del peregrino**" (Pilgrim's Our Father) is a prayer of unknown origin. It appeared in the book *En torno al Padrenuestro* (Narcea 1999) and is posted in the church of Santiago el Real in Logroño, Spain.

"**Peregrino**" (Pilgrim) is by **Luis Cernuda** (1902-1963), a poet from Seville, Spain. The poem first appeared in *Desolación de la Quimera* (1962). © Herederos de Luis Cernuda, reprinted with permission.

"**Peregrinos a Santiago**" (Pilgrims to Santiago) is a poem that appears on a wall near Nájera, La Rioja, Spain. **Eugenio Garibay Baños** (1932-2018) wrote the poem in 1987. He was a parish priest who helped rebuild and promote the Camino. He also loved to tell stories and sign cards displaying this poem.

"**Pilgrim**" is a song by **John Mark McMillan** (b. 1979), a singer/songwriter from Charlotte, North Carolina, USA. The song comes from "Peopled with Dreams" (2020) and the lyrics are included with permission.

"**Pilgrim Blessing**" was written by **Macrina Wiederkehr** (1939-2020), a Catholic sister, author, and educator at St. Scholastica Monastery in Fort Smith, Arkansas, USA. The prayer appeared in Joyce Rupp's book, *Walk in a Relaxed Manner* (Orbis 2005). and it is reprinted with permission.

"**Pilgrim's Credo**" is a prayer by **Murray Bodo**, OFM (b. 1937), a Franciscan priest in Cincinnati, Ohio, USA. It was written in Rye, England, after completing a pilgrimage to Assisi and appears in *The Road to Mount Subasio* (Tau 2011). It is included with permission.

"**A Prayer among Friends**" is a poem by **John Daniel** (b. 1948), an author and educator who lives near Eugene, Oregon, USA. The poem appeared in *Of Earth: New and Selected Poems* (Lost Horse Press 2012) and is included with permission.

**"Prayer for Nature"** was composed by **Nachman of Breslov** (1772-1810), a Hasidic Jewish rabbi from Ukraine.

**"Prayer for the Time of Sunrise"** is a prayer by **Kevin A. Codd** (b. 1953), a Catholic priest serving in Spokane, Washington, USA. The prayer appeared in his book, *To the Field of Stars: A Pilgrim's Journey to Santiago de Compostela* (Eerdmans 2008). It is included with permission.

**"Prayer for Travelers"** and its translation are by **Angela Herrera** (b.1976), Senior Minister at First Unitarian Church in Albuquerque, New Mexico, USA. The prayer appears in *Reaching for the Sun* (Skinner House 2012) and it is reprinted with permission.

**"Proverbios y cantares XXIX"** (Proverbs and Songs 29) was written by **Antonio Machado** (1875-1939), a poet from Seville, Spain. It first appeared in *Campos de Castilla* (Madrid Renacimiento 1912). The translation, included with permission, is by **Betty Jean Craige** (b. 1946), who was a professor at the University of Georgia (USA). The poem became part of "Cantares" (1969), a song by Joan Manuel Serrat.

**"The Road Not Taken"** is by **Robert Frost** (1874-1963), a US poet who is most identified with New England. The poem first appeared in *Mountain Interval* (Holt 1916).

**"The Road to Santiago"** is a song by **Heather M. Dale** (b. 1974), a Celtic music recording artist based in Toronto, Ontario, Canada (https://heatherdale.com/). The song appeared on her album "The Road to Santiago" (Amphis Music 2005). The lyrics are included with permission.

**"Santiago"** is a song by **David Wilcox** (b. 1958), a folk musician based in Asheville, North Carolina, USA. It appears on "'The View From the Edge." ©2018 David Wilcox, published by Gizz Da Baboo (SESAC), administered by Michelle Ma Soeur (SESAC), a division of Soroka Music Ltd. All rights reserved. Reprinted with permission.

**"Santiago: balada ingenua"** (St. James: Naïve Ballad) is a poem by **Federico García Lorca** (1898-1936), a Spanish poet and playwright from Granada, Spain. Lorca wrote the poem at the age of 20 on the feast day of St. James and it debuted in *Libro de Poemas* (Hernández Sánchez 1921).

**"The Song of Amergin"** is attributed to **Amergin Glúingel**, a mythical Milesian bard. This invocation of the spirit of Ireland may be the oldest poem from the British Isles. The translation by Lady Gregory August comes from *Gods and Fighting Men* (1904) and I included a final line found in other versions.

**"Song of the Open Road, 1"** is part of a poem by **Walt Whitman** (1819-1892), a poet, essayist, and journalist who lived in Brooklyn, New York, USA. The poem debuted in *Leaves of Grass* (Rome 1856).

**"Song of the Sky Loom"** is a **Tewa song** of the Pueblo Native American people of Arizona, USA. Translated by Herbert Joseph Spinden, it appeared in *Songs of the Tewa* (1933).

**"Today"** is a prayer by the Persian poet **Hafiz** (1315-1390). This translation by **Daniel Ladinsky** is from his book, *A Year With Hafiz: Daily Contemplations* (Penguin 2011). Mr. Ladinsky (b. 1948) is a poet from St. Louis, Missouri, USA. The text is used with permission.

**"Traveler's Prayer"** (Tefilat HaDerech) is a **Jewish prayer** from *The Talmud*, Berakhot 29b:17. The English wording is from the William Davidson digital edition of *The Koren Noé Talmud*.

**"Walking in Beauty"** is part of a prayer from the Night Chant ceremony of the **Navajo**, a Native American people of the southwestern USA. The prayer appeared in *The Path of the Rainbow* (Boni & Liveright 1918).

**"Walking the Way"** was written for this book by **Salvatore Sapienza** (b. 1964), pastor of the Douglas (Michigan, USA) Congregational United Church of Christ and author of several books. Pastor Sal earned his *Compostela* in 2019.

**"The Wayfaring Pilgrim"** is an American folk and gospel song from before 1860. It is also called "Wayfaring Stranger."

**"With Every Breath"** is a Buddhist prayer of unknown authorship.

**"You are the Journey"** is a paraphrase of a prayer by **St. Severinus Boethius** (480-524), a Roman senator and philosopher. The text is from an influential work, *The Consolation of Philosophy*.

# Additional Works

I could not include everything that I would have liked in this book. Here are a few items that you might enjoy exploring.

**"A Prayer for the World"**
> Rabbi Harold Kushner in *Parade Magazine*, March 2003:
> "Let the warmth of the sun heal us wherever we are broken."

**"Camino"**
> David Whyte's poem from *Pilgrim* (2012):
> "other people seemed to know you even before you gave up being a shadow on the road."

**"For the Traveler"**
> John O'Donohue's blessing from *To Bless the Space Between Us* (2008): "a new silence goes with you, and if you listen, you will hear what your heart would love to say."

**"I Have No Idea Where I Am Going"**
> Thomas Merton's prayer from *Thoughts in Solitude* (1956):
> "I do not see the road ahead of me. I cannot know for certain where it will end."

**"i thank You God"**
> e e cummings' work from *Poems, 1923-1954*:
> "this is the birth day of life and love and wings;"

**"I'm Going to Go Back There Someday"**
> Paul Williams and Kenny Ascher's song from "The Muppet Movie" (1979):
> "There's not a word yet for old friends who've just met.
> Part heaven, part space, or have I found my place?"

**"The Call"**
> Regina Spektor's song from "The Chronicles of Narnia: Prince Caspian" (2008):
> "Pick a star on the dark horizon and follow the light. You'll come back when it's over; no need to say goodbye."

### "The Journey"

Mary Oliver's poem from *Dream Work* (2014):
"the stars began to burn through the sheets of clouds, and there was a new voice which you slowly recognized as your own."

### "Pilgrim"

Enya's song from "A Day Without Rain" (2000):
"pilgrim it's a long way to find out who you are."

### "Questions for the Angels"

Paul Simon's song from "So Beautiful or So What" (2011):
"Who believes in angels?
Fools and pilgrims all over the world."

# Acknowledgments

**More than twenty authors** generously allowed their work to be included here without compensation. *Se lo agradezco.*

**Rev. Salvatore Sapienza**, pastor at Douglas UCC, encouraged me to make the effort to publish this book, then added a wonderful contribution. *Dios te bendiga.*

**Doug Haberland**, a friend and former colleague with experience in magazine editing, proofread the book and provided expert feedback. *Vaya donde vaya . . .*

**José Luis Martínez Massa,** a *madrileño* who has been my friend for nearly fifty years, provided extensive and invaluable help with the translations. *¡Viva la YMCA!*

**Dr. Karen Clark** supported me all the way. She is my wife of 43 years, mother and grandmother to my progeny, loving critic, counselor, and best friend. *Te quiero.*

Chris Clark
Fennville, Michigan, USA
https://www.gchrisclark.com